F is for Fiji!

By: Latoya Beatty

Author
Latoya Beatty

B & G Publishing

It's been a long, hot summer and I've been planning my next adventure!

I've been planning to go some place tropical with lots of things to get into.

I've heard about a place that's as beautiful as can be. There have even been commercials about it all over the T.V!

I decided to listen closely and see where it could be. I watched and listened, watched and listened.......

We're going to Fiji!

Flying over Fiji was a beautiful sight to see.

The ocean was beautiful see-through water, and there were lots of beautiful green palm trees!

The sun was shining bright, and there was not a cloud in the sky.

I knew right away it would be hard to say goodbye!

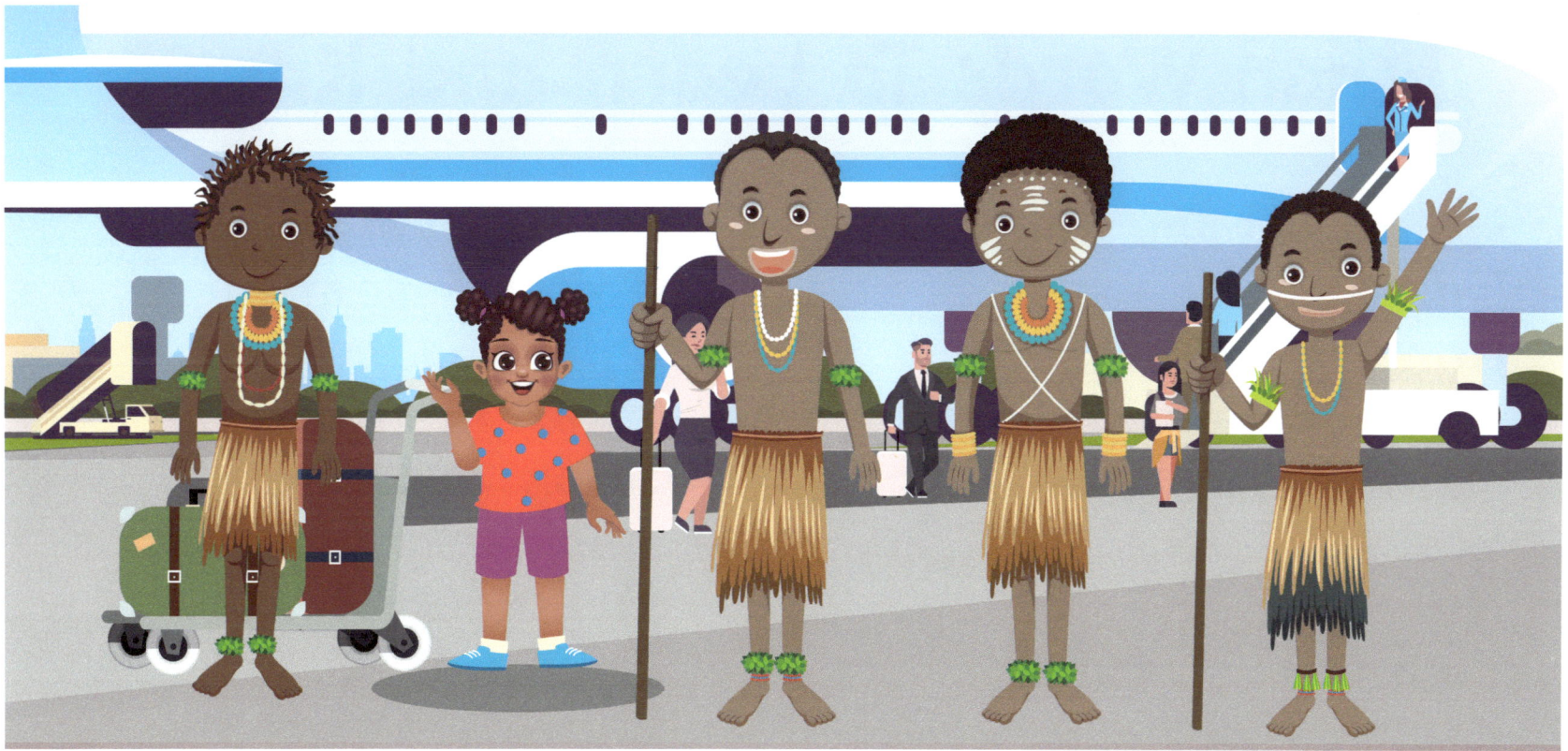

When I landed in Fiji I noticed right away,

Their language there was different and I wanted to learn it during my stay!

The languages spoken there are Fijian, English, and Fiji Hindi.

I didn't realize there would be so many!

The first word I picked up was how to say hello.

Hello in Fijian is Bula, and

Excuse me is Tolou!

Fijian Words To Learn and Know!

- **Hello:** *Ni sa bula* or just *bula*
- **Goodbye:** *Ni sa moce*
- **Good Morning:** *Ni sa yadra*
- **Yes:** *Lo*
- **No:** *Sega*
- **Please:** *Yalo vinaka*
- **Excuse me:** *Tolou*
- **Thank you / good:** *Vinaka*
- **Thank you very much:** *Vinaka vaka levu*
- **What is this?:** *A cava oqo?*
- **It's a...:** *E dua na...*
- **House:** *Vale* or *bure*
- **Man:** *Tagane*

- **Woman:** *marama*
- **Toilet:** *Vale lailai*
- **Village:** *Koro*
- **Church:** *Vale ni lotu*
- **Shop:** *Sitoa*
- **Eat:** *Kana*
- **Drink:** *Gunu*
- **Coconut:** *Niu*
- **Quickly:** *Vaka totolo*
- **Big:** *Levu*
- **Small:** *Lailai*
- **Slowly:** *Vaka malua*
- **A little/small:** *Vaka lailai*
- **A lot/great:** *Vaka levee*
- **One:** *Dua*
- **Two:** *Rua*

Fire Walking Ceremony

I was ready to explore, so I went out to find fun things to do.

I was looking forward to trying something new!

It was exciting to see a Fire Walking ceremony, and I swam with

manta rays too!

Swimming With Manta Rays!

Lovo Chicken

After having so much fun I needed to get something to eat.

Since I was in a new country I wanted something different and unique!

I learned about the Fijian Lovo meal, and I couldn't wait to eat!

I had chicken and I had fish,

It was all wrapped in banana leaves!

The food was prepared in an underground oven and the hole was covered with dirt until it was smoking hot!

I'm sure you can imagine I enjoyed that meal quite a lot!

I also tried Rourou and Cassava chips. The Rourou was made with Taro leaves and stewed in coconut milk!

The Cassava chips are not the kind you eat with dip! It was amazing to try and very hard to resist!

Underground Oven

Cassava Chips

Rourou

Lovo Fish

Fiji Crested Iguana

After trying many different kinds of foods I wanted to go out and do more exploring!

There was so much beautiful wildlife to see, my adventure was never boring!

I saw the Fiji Crested Iguana and the Fijian Monkey-Faced Bat! That was a sight to see! I didn't think there would be anything topping that!

But......

I saw the Orange Fruit Dove and the Red-Throated Lorikeet! Both of those birds are amazingly beautiful and unique! What more was there to see!

Red-Throated Lorikeet!

Orange Fruit Dove!

Fijian Monkey-Faced Bat!

Fiji Airport

My trip to Fiji was an unforgettable adventure!
I learned so many new things and found a lot to get into!
I hope our next adventure comes around soon!
Hey, you never know, we might go to the moon!
Until our next Big Adventure!

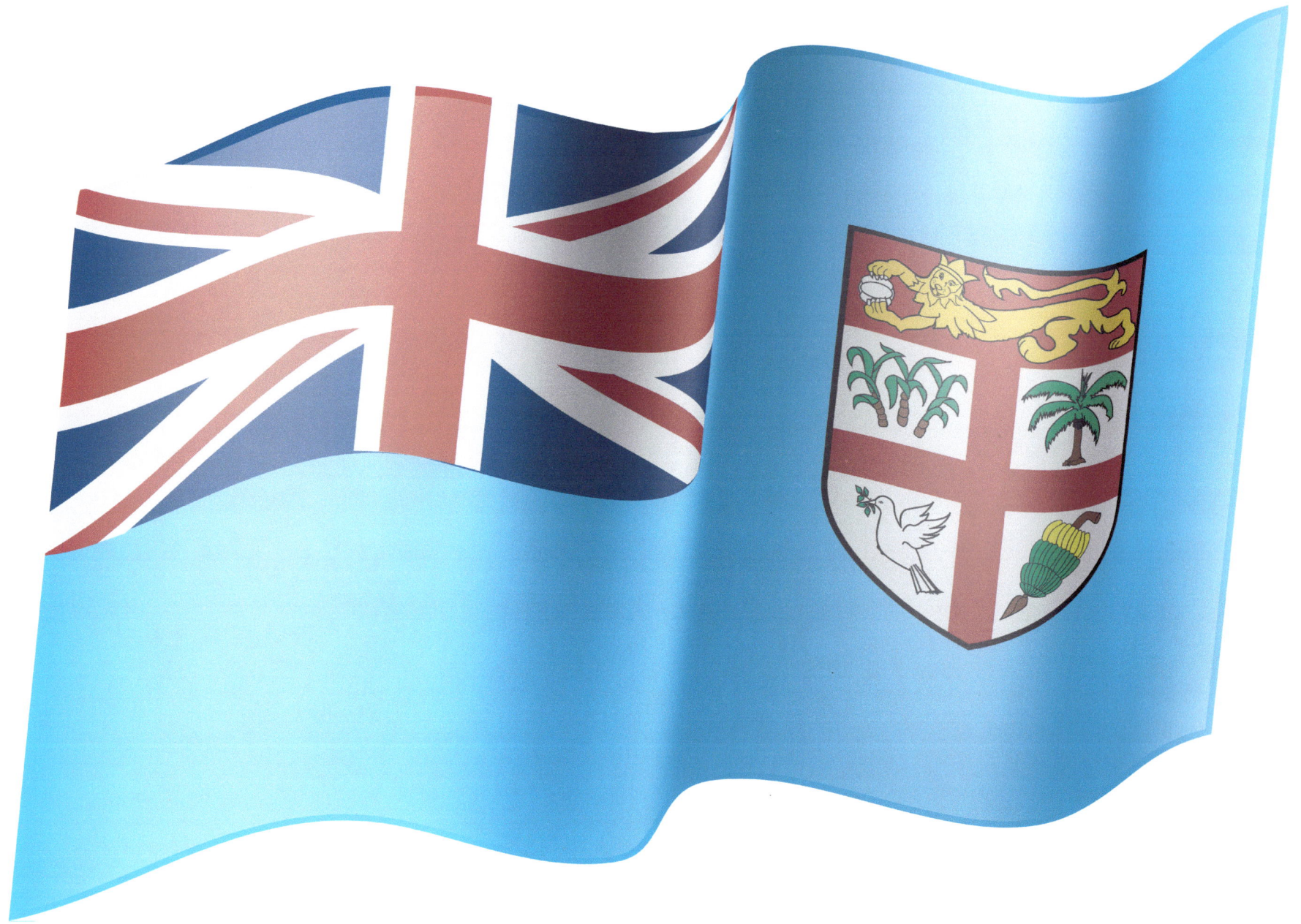

Fiji

Let's See What You've Learned!

What Dish Is This?

What Animal Is This?

What Dish Is This?

What Animal Is This?

What Dish Is This?

What Animal Is This?

What Is She Doing?

What Ceremony Is This?

Great Job!

For Jayden, DJ, Princess,
PJ, RJ, Caelyn, Nadia,
Austin, and Illiana.

For all the wonderful children at

Little Pandas Child Care Center

in Martinsburg, WV

www.pandaschildcare.com

B & G Publishing

www.ingramcontent.com/pod-product-compliance
Lightning Source LLC
Chambersburg PA
CBHW040405100426

42811CB00017B/1846